"Kama Sutra is the delight of the senses and its object is to attain the peak of pleasure. Man should practice Kama Sutra in all the different stages of his long life."

Kama Sutra Book II

MAYA
SUTRA

First Edition: Editorial Dante / Mérida, 2001 / ISBN: 970 605 267 4/ Cover design: Soraya Ciprés Re /
Illustrations:Javier Covo Torres / ©️ 2001. Javier Covo Torres / Editorial Dante, s.a. de c. v / Calle 17 nº 138b /
C.P.97100 / Mérida, Yucatán, México / Impreso en México / Printed in México

INTRODUCTION

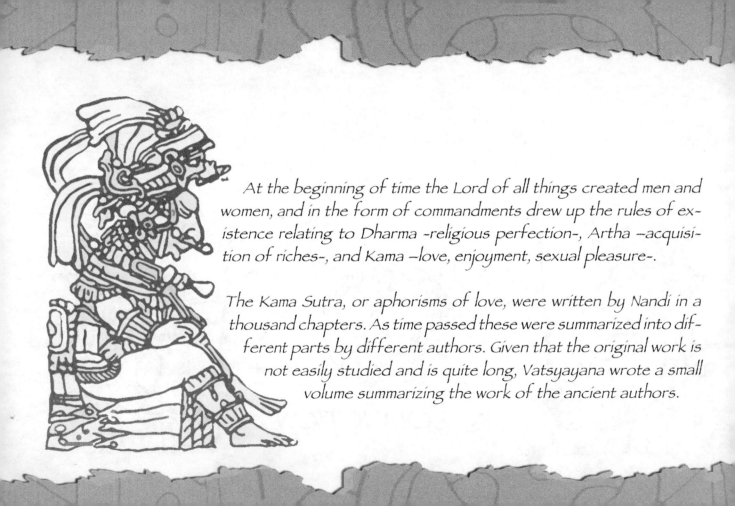

At the beginning of time the Lord of all things created men and women, and in the form of commandments drew up the rules of existence relating to Dharma -religious perfection-, Artha -acquisition of riches-, and Kama -love, enjoyment, sexual pleasure-.

The Kama Sutra, or aphorisms of love, were written by Nandi in a thousand chapters. As time passed these were summarized into different parts by different authors. Given that the original work is not easily studied and is quite long, Vatsyayana wrote a small volume summarizing the work of the ancient authors.

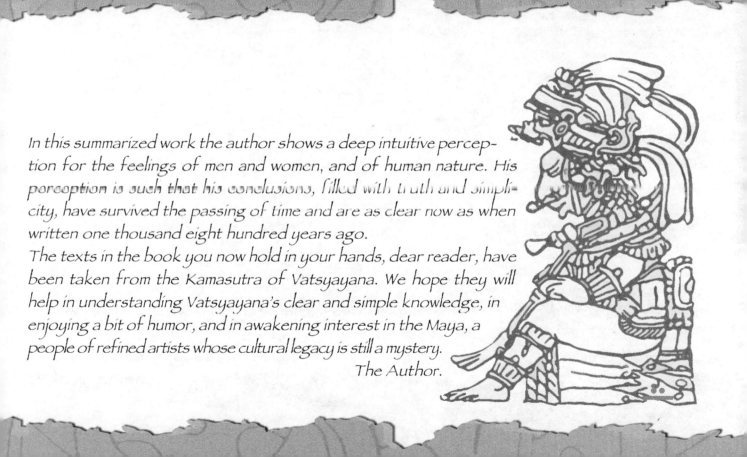

In this summarized work the author shows a deep intuitive perception for the feelings of men and women, and of human nature. His perception is such that his conclusions, filled with truth and simplicity, have survived the passing of time and are as clear now as when written one thousand eight hundred years ago.

The texts in the book you now hold in your hands, dear reader, have been taken from the Kamasutra of Vatsyayana. We hope they will help in understanding Vatsyayana's clear and simple knowledge, in enjoying a bit of humor, and in awakening interest in the Maya, a people of refined artists whose cultural legacy is still a mystery.

The Author.

Pleasures are necessary for the body's existence and well-being. The man who practices Kama Sutra enjoys happiness in this life and the next. Good citizens will carry out acts that do not inspire fear in life and do not damage their well-being.

Kamasutra. Book II

ADOPTING KAMA SUTRA

KNOWLEDGE OF KAMA SUTRA

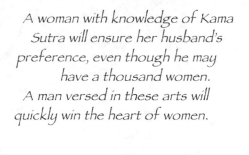

A woman with knowledge of Kama
Sutra will ensure her husband's
preference, even though he may
have a thousand women.
A man versed in these arts will
quickly win the heart of women.

Young people should
study Kama Sutra.
Women should do it
before marriage so as to
continue studying with the
consent of their husbands.

STUDY OF THE ARTS AND SCIENCES

Song and musical instruments.
The art of divining a man's character from his physiognomy.
The art of making a bed on which to lay.
The making of necklaces and wreathes.
The colors of jewels and precious stones
Arrangement of turbans and headdresses.
Preparation of perfumes and essences.
Agility of the hands, magic.
The culinary arts.
Coloring the teeth and nails.
The art of mimicry.
Tattoos.
The art of applying perfumed ointments to the body.
The art of infusing the hair with aroma.
Drawing and reading.

A learned man of good fortune will lead the life of a citizen. He will take a house in a good location and surround it with gardens. He will have a house only for women with rooms anointed with rich perfumes, a bed covered with a canopy of wreaths and flowers and a patio with birdcages under a roof covered with climbing plants.

Awakening in the morning he will apply ointments and color to his lips and eyelashes. He will breakfast and occupy himself teaching the parrots to speak. Accompanied by women, he will bathe in water completely

OF A CITIZEN

surrounded by rocks from which all dangerous
animals have been removed.

After a rest he will don clothes and adornments,
and spend the afternoon with friends, cel-
ebrating spring, catching flowers, eating
mango fruit and tender ears of corn.

He will spend the night playing dice or strolling in
the moonlight. When the night is over, he will wait
in his decorated and perfumed room for the arrival
of the woman who will make him happy.

THE KISS

"All things that one lover does to the other, whatever they be, should be reciprocated: if the woman kisses the man, he should kiss her in return, if she spanks him, he should spank her..."

Kama Sutra. Book III

TS'UTS'

KULCHE'
(THE STATUE)

NOMINAL KISS

This is when a maiden touches the mouth of her lover with her mouth, without moving or doing anything, just feeling the delicate touch of her lips against his.

Kama Sutra. Book III

THROBBING KISS

"When a young woman, forgetting modesty, wants to touch the lips that push against her mouth, and to do so moves her lower but not her upper lip, this is the throbbing kiss".

Kama Sutra. Book III

I'M NOT QUITE SURE

WHERE I'M THROBBING...

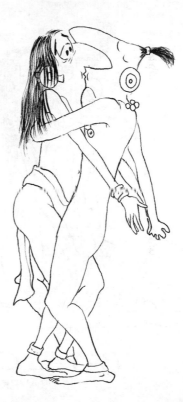

PEK
(THE THROBBING)

PAYAL CHI'
(THE PRAYER)

TOUCHING KISS

"When a young woman touches her lover's lips with her tongue, closes her eyes, pushes her breasts against his chest and puts her hands on his, this is the touching kiss".

Kama Sutra. Book III

THE KISSING IS THE LEAST OF IT, WHAT MATTERS IS THE "TOUCHING"

INCLINED KISS

"When the heads of both lovers are inclined one toward the other and they kiss, this is the inclined kiss".

Kama Sutra. Book III

THERE'S ONE TWISTED DETAIL:

THE CRICK IN YOUR NECK.

MANAK'
(THE STELE)

PAY KISIN
(THE IDOLATER)

STRETCHING KISS

"When one of the lovers takes the other by the hair, face, chin or cheeks, holds their head and brings it toward him or her, it is called the stretching kiss".

Kama Sutra. Book III

CAREFUL WITH THE HAIR

WOULDN'T WANT TO BE MISTAKEN FOR AN APACHE

MOSON

(THE WHIRLWIND)

- 21 -

TS'AL
(THE SEAL)

PRESSURE KISS

"When one of the lovers strongly presses against the lower lip of the other, it is, undoubtedly, a pressure kiss".

Kama Sutra. Book III

HIGH PRESSURE KISS

"Done by holding the woman's lower lip with the fingers while running the other hand down her back. She is caressed with the tongue while her lip is held and she is given a soft bite to increase the pleasure".

Kama Sutra. Book III

PETS'
(THE PRESS)

K'AK'
(THE BONFIRE)

THE KISS THAT REVIVES

"When the lover is sleeping, for example, and his woman comes to let him know she would like to be taken, this is the reviving kiss".

Kama Sutra. Book III

SUM

(THE JUGGLER)

- 25 -

P'IX ICH
(THE INSOMNIAC)

THE KISS THAT AWAKENS

If the lover arrives at his loved one's house in the early morning, and kisses her to let her know his desire and the pleasure he hopes have with her, this is called the kiss that awakens.

Kama Sutra. Book III

NEXT TIME I LET HER SLEEP

...I SWEAR

THE KISS THAT IGNITES

"These are kisses between the thighs and the bellybutton, kisses that make the woman feel desired, full of pleasure and satisfied even before coupling".

Kama Sutra. Book III

P'ILIS
(THE SPARK)

PES
(THE DEMONSTRATION)

DEMONSTRA-TIVE KISS

"When at night, in the theater or a party, a man comes to a woman and kisses one of her fingers, if she is stand-ing, or one of her toes, if she is sitting, this is a demonstrative kiss."

Kama Sutra. Book III

"A demonstrative kiss, meant to inflame passion, is also when a woman, pushing on her lover's body, puts her face on his thigh as if she wants to sleep, and kisses his thigh or the big toe of his foot."

Kama Sutra. Book III

THE EMBRACE

"The embrace is another way of awakening desire. There are embraces that are not mentioned in the Kama Sutra and that should be practiced at the moment of sexual pleasure, because the rules of the Kama Sutra are open when the wheel of love begins to spin."

Kama Sutra. Book II

TAK'AL
(THE GROPE)

TOUCHING EMBRACE

"When a man, under one pretext or another, puts himself in front of, or to one side of, the woman he desires or loves, and touches her with his body, this is the touching embrace".

Kama Sutra. Book II

...BUT IT WAS WORTH IT...

RUBBING EMBRACE

"When lovers stroll alone at night, in the darkness, in public or in isolated couples, and passionately rub against one another, this is a rubbing embrace".

Kama Sutra, Book II

I PREFER "SCRATCHING" INSTEAD OF "RUBBING"

HII'

(RUBBING)

HEP'
(THE SQUEEZE)

REPTILE EMBRACE

"When the woman grabs her lover like a reptile grabs a tree, brings her head to his to kiss him, looks at him lovingly and sighs, it is called a reptile embrace".

Kama Sutra. Book II

XAKNAL
(THE REPTILE)

EB

(THE STAIR)

CLIMBING THE TREE

"With one foot on his foot and the other on his thigh, the woman puts one arm around his kidneys and the other around his shoulders while she coos at him that she wants to climb up him for a kiss".

Kama Sutra. Book II

MILK AND WATER EMBRACE

"This is when the lovers' desire is violent and uncontrolled, and they embrace as if to melt into one. This is the case when the woman is between the man's legs, against a column, or lying on the bed".
(Kama Sutra. Book II)

K'ALAB
(THE LOCK)

WAYTANIL
(WITCHCRAFT)

WELL WATER IN A GOURD
(MAYA LOVE POTION)

THIGH EMBRACE

"This is when one of the lovers presses one or both of the others thighs between theirs".

Kama Sutra. Book II

LAP

(THE HOOK)

NEK´
(THE SEED)

GROIN EMBRACE

"This is when the man pushes his groin against the woman's, and climbs on her to scratch, hit, bite, caress or kiss her while her hair blows in the wind".

Kama Sutra. Book II

EMBRACE OF THE BREASTS

"When the man strongly embraces his lover and pushes his chest against her breasts, this is called the embrace of the breasts".

MUKÚL
(THE SECRET)

HEEP'
(THE COMPRESS)

COMPRESSING EMBRACE

"If the lovers legs are extended and in mutual contact, this is called the compressed embrace"

Kama Sutra. Book II

PUCHH AH
(THE CRUSH)

SESAME AND RICE

"This is when the lovers tightly embrace, strongly intertwining their arms and legs".

Kama Sutra. Book II

"All women, discrete, simple or self-confident, if they show
their love outwardly, can be easily won".

Kama Sutra. Book V, Chapter II

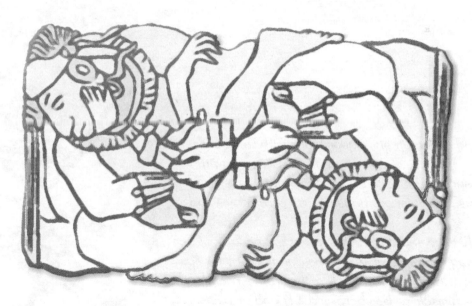

WAYS OF APPROACHING A WOMAN

The man should strike up an acquaintance with the loved
woman in the following way:
He should be sure to be seen by her on all occasions; in a
friend's house, a minister's house, floral ceremonies and
festivals.
When he meets her, he should bite her lower lip and look at her
in such a way that she will guess the condition of his spirit.
When she looks at him, he should talk of her to his friends, show
himself to be liberal and a friend of pleasure.

Everything should be done at a convenient time and place. When the young woman is no longer modest, they will buy clothing, garlands and rings together. He will ask her for one of the flowers in her hair and will leave the soft aroma of the flower marked with his teeth. When alone, he will embrace and kiss her. When a man is to seduce a woman, he should never seduce another at the same time".

Kama Sutra. Book V, Chapter II

GOOD QUALITIES IN A MAN

"For love, women will search for men with excellent qualities:
Highborn men.
Worldly men.
Tellers of beautiful stories.
Energetic men with training in the arts and knowledge of the hereafter.
Men without anger.
Men who enjoy parties.
Men with robust bodies.
Men who do not drink, and are indefatigable in the exercise of love.
Men who give their hearts to women without totally surrendering themselves.
Men with the means to subsist independently.
Men without envy.

GOOD QUALITIES IN A WOMAN

A woman should distinguish herself with the following qualities:
She should be beautiful and amiable.
She should love the good qualities of others.
She should delight in sexual union that comes from love.
She should try to equal the man in sexual enjoyment.
She should always wish to acquire experience.
She should live without avarice.
She should enjoy parties and the arts.
She should be intelligent, well-mannered, of regular behavior and agreeable character.
She should use correct language without a mocking grin or maliciousness.
She should not be covetous, silly or stupid.
She should know the Kama Sutra and be trained in the arts of love."

Kama Sutra. Book V, Chapter 1

MEN WHO ARE LUCKY WITH WOMEN

Men who generally obtain the favors of women are:
Those very versed in the science of love.
Those who give gifts.
Those who have not loved other women before.
Those who are desired by honorable women.
Those given to sexual pleasure.
Those of liberal character.
Those who are valiant and strong.
Those who dress and live splendidly.
Those of good appearance.
Those who inspire confidence and familiarity.
Those who can easily tell stories.

WOMEN WHO ARE EASY TO OBTAIN

Those who always look towards the street.
Those who spend their time at a neighbor's house.
Those who constantly look at men.
She who looks to one side.
She who hates her husband.
Those who have not had children.
Those who are apparently in love with their husbands.
Those who love pleasures.
Those presumptuous of their skills in the arts.
She who is badly treated by her husband.
She whose husband spends time traveling.
Those who are jealous.".

Kama Sutra. Book V, Chapter I

THE SPIRITUAL CONDITION OF A WOMAN

A woman who allows herself to be courted, but does yield with time,
may be tricky in love, but can be won by staying close to her.
When a woman avoids the attention of the man and rejects him with hard words,
he should retire from the battlefield and abandon it forever.
When a woman rejects a man but simultaneously shows affection in her actions,
should be made love to as soon as possible.
When a woman offers an opportunity to a man and tells him she loves him,
it is his sacred duty to enjoy her.

HOW WOMEN EXPRESS LOVE

A woman expresses love in various ways:
    She addresses the man without his having spoken to her first.
    She appears in secret places.
    Her fingers moisten with perspiration.
    She shows the radiant appearance of pleasure.
    She trembles in front of the man.
    She speaks inarticulately.
    She touches her body and squeezes her head.
    She lets her hands fall on her body, as if exhausted.

THE SCRATCH

"The love of a woman who has signs of scratches on her body, though they may be old and almost invisible, can be reactivated and renewed. Without these marks of love, the love diminishes as when much time has passed without coupling.

Kama Sutra. Book II, Chapter IV

"The first visit, when lying with the woman for the first time.

...when the lover is drunk, inebriated, intoxicated.

FOR SCRATCHING

When two angry lovers reconcile. It is a sign of wanting to possess each other again, helping them believe that nothing has happened.

When the lover travels, he makes a mark on the chest, breasts or thighs of the loved one. Three or four lines together, made with the nails, is enough to leave an unforgettable memory."

Kama Sutra. Book II, Chapter IV

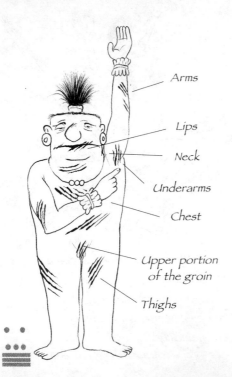

Arms

Lips

Neck

Underarms

Chest

Upper portion
of the groin

Thighs

PLACES TO LEAVE MARKS WITH THE NAILS

"When the passion is impetuous, do not worry about the place."

Kama Sutra. Book II, Chapter IV

THE EIGHT CLASSES
OF SCRATCH

There are eight classes of nail pressure, ordered
according to the marks they produce.

- 59 -

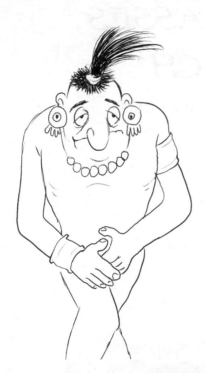

PET

(CIRCLE)

CIRCLE

"Done on the neck and other places, it is also known as "moon shadow". It is a mark that takes much time to go away".

Kama Sutra. Book II

HALF CIRCLE

"Known as the "half moon", this mark is left on the buttocks and around the bellybutton."

Kama Sutra. Book II

UH

(MOON)

T'OL

(LINE)

LINE

"This is a short scratch,
with almost no trace of
the nail mark, but can
appear on any part of
the body."

Kama Sutra. Book II

TIGER CLAW

"This is a deep line on the chest that can reach to below the bellybutton. The tiger claw is a sign of great enjoyment for lovers."

Kama Sutra. Book II

I DON'T LIKE THIS FANTASY ANYMORE...

MO'L
(TIGER CLAW))

- 63 -

TSO'

(PEACOCK)

PEACOCK CLAW

"This mark is presumptuous and vane. It is made on the chest with five fingernails, of an equal length, with equal space between the scratches. Lots of practice is required for this fete."

Kama Sutra. Book II

JUMPING HARE

"This mark is made around the nipple of the loved one, with the five fingernails, while kissing her or caressing her with the other hand. It produces stinging and pain, but also the sensation of pleasure and the desire to be possessed."

Kama Sutra. Book II

HE'S USELESS LOOK,

HE LEFT OFF ONE OF THE SCRATCHES.

TSUB

(HARE)

KI

(MAGUEY)

BLUE LOTUS LEAF

"This is a mark on the chest of the man or the breasts of the woman, in the form of a blue lotus leaf."

Kama Sutra. Book II

AT LEAST IT'S NOT IN THE SHAPE OF PALM TREE

FIRM PRESSURE

"This is when a person presses on the chin, lower lip, breasts, or groin of another, so sweetly that it only leaves a slight mark. This is done with a young woman when her lover wants to stir her up or scare her. The mark is easily erased."

Kama Sutra. Book II

K'AX

(FOREST)

THE BITE

"During the day, in a busy place, if her lover shows some sign of his teeth, she will smile and, turning her head in an irritated way, will show him the marks he left on her body".

Kama Sutra. Book II, Chapter V

CHI'BAL

PIX

(HIDDEN BITE)

HIDDEN BITE

This is when, in excessive passion and desire, one softly bites the left cheek of the lover, leaving a mark that lasts just as long as the love-making.

Kama Sutra. Book II

SWOLLEN BITE

"This is when the bite reddens the skin, swells and leaves teeth marks. When the bite makes one almost scream from pleasure and pain, this is the swollen bite."

Kama Sutra. Book II

WELL, I BIT HIM WITH MY MOLARS

AND I'D JUST HAD A ROOT CANAL

KU CHUPU
(SWOLLEN BITE)

71 -

NI'
(THE POINT)

THE POINT

"When the woman is
bitten on the arm,
thighs or joint of
the thighs, it is
called the point".
Kama Sutra. Book II

MY
SPECIALTY
IS

"THE
POINT"

CORAL AND JEWEL

"This bite is made on the body of a woman using both the lips and teeth. The coral is the mark of the lips and the jewel that of the teeth".

Kama Sutra, Book II

I'LL STICK WITH THE CORAL THE JEWEL HURTS

LOL
(FLOWER)

AH K'ANTIXAL
(THE JEWEL)

BROKEN CLOUD

"This is a bite given on the breasts, and whose marks make a partial or unequal circle around the nipple, caused by the separation between the teeth".

Kama Sutra, Book II

K'UYEN
(THE SACRILEGE)

SACPECH
(THE LEECH)

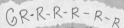

LINE OF JEWELS

"When the lover is bitten with all the teeth, leaving the skin red, this is the line of jewels".

Kama Sutra. Book II

KITAM
(WILD BOAR)

WILD BOAR

"This is a bite that leaves red marks, one next to the other, on the breasts and back. It is an option for intensely passionate people, and because of this is given in the seconds before coitus, when coupling has begun."

Kama Sutra. Book II

"The different classes of coupling, practiced according to the particular fantasy of each individual, can create love, sincere friendship and real respect in the heart of women".

Kama Sutra. Book II, Chapter I

COUPLING BY MEASURES

Men are classified in three ways
according to their KEP:

MAN – HARE
MAN – BULL
MAN – HORSE

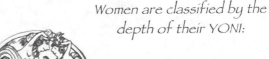

Women are classified by the
depth of their YONI:

WOMAN – DEER
WOMAN – DONKEY
WOMAN – ELEPHANT

EQUAL COUPLINGS

The best couplings are between persons with corresponding measurements:
HARE – DEER; BULL – DONKEY; HORSE – ELEPHANT

HIGH COUPLING
LOW COUPLING
(Medium quality couplings)

A high coupling is when the
dimensions of the man are
larger than those of the woman:
HORSE – DONKEY
BULL – DEER

A low coupling occurs when the
inverse is true:
ELEPHANT – BULL
DONKEY – HARE

VERY HIGH COUPLING
VERY LOW COUPLING
(The worst couplings)

Very high couplings are
between the man with the
largest measurements
and the woman with the
smallest:
HORSE – DEER

Very low couplings occur
when the inverse is true:
ELEPHANT – HARE

COUPLING ACCORDING TO PASSION

"A man has little passion when his desire is not ignited at the moment of coupling and he cannot tolerate the fiery embraces of the woman.

Men of medium passion are of a better temperament.

Those in the grips of desire are men of intense passion.

Men and women are categorized into three durations of passion:

Those of little duration; those of moderate duration and those of long duration".

Kama Sutra. Book II

COUPLING ACCORDING TO DESIRE

The first time coupling occurs, the man's passion is
intense and the duration is short. But the contrary is true
of the following couplings the same day: the passion is low,
but the duration is longer.

This occurs differently in the woman because her passion is
weak the first time and the duration is long. In the following
couplings on the same day, however, her desire is intense and
the her duration is short; until she is completely satisfied".

Kama Sutra. Book II

DIFFERENT WAYS OF COUPLING

"An ingenious person will multiply the classes of couplings by imitating the different species of beasts and birds. These classes of coupling can create love, sincere friendship and real respect in the heart of women."

Kama Sutra. Book II, Chapter VI

TSAYAMHAL

PETS'

(COMPRESS)

TIGHT POSITION

"If the woman squeezes the man with her thighs, it is known as the tight position".
Kama Sutra. Book II

ELEVATED POSITION

If the woman elevates her thighs, keeping her legs completely separate, it is called the elevated position".

Kama Sutra. Book II

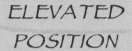

SAK'
(THE LOBSTER)

TAB

(ENTWINE)

ENTWINED
POSITION

"This is when the woman lifts her legs and holds the man's legs with them, raising her waist and then putting one of her thighs over that of her lover, leaving the other thigh where it is".

Kama Sutra. Book II

CRAB POSITION

"This is when the woman's legs, separated, are placed on her stomach for coupling".

Kama Sutra. Book II

(IX) BAW
(THE CRAB)

TEP'
(PACKAGE)

PACKAGE POSITION

"When the thighs are placed one over the other, this is the package position".
Kama Sutra. Book II

"WITH LOVE ...DICK"

THE LITTLE PACKAGE

SETTING
THE NAIL

"When the woman puts her leg over the head of her lover and extends the other, this is setting the nail. It can be learned with practice".

Kama Sutra, Book II

KEP MASKAB
(THE NAIL)

CH'UPUL WAKAX

(THE COW)

THE COW

"When the woman, with her back to her lover, supports her hands and keeps her feet on the ground, and her lover mounts hers, this is called the cow".

Kama Sutra. Book II

AH' XIMBAL

(THE WALKER)

OPENING BAMBOO

"This is when the woman puts one of her legs over the man's shoulder and extends the other leg. She then places the extended leg over the other shoulder, alternating movements one after the other until reaching total union with the man".

Kama Sutra. Book II

- 93 -

HOKOB
(THE HOOK)

VERY OPEN POSITION

This is when the woman, once lying down, lowers her head, and raises her body from the waist down, keeping her feet on the bed".

Kama Sutra. Book II

SINA'N

(THE SCORPION)

K'I'IX OCH
(THE HEDGEHOG)

MODERATELY PRESSING POSITION

"When, during coupling, the woman extends one of her legs while raising the other to place it on the bed, this is the moderately pressing position".

Kama Sutra. Book II

PRESSING POSITION

"This is when the woman contracts her legs and her lover takes them in his hands and presses them against her chest"

Kama Sutra. Book II

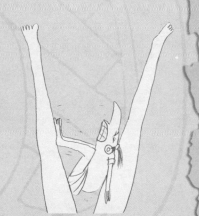

TS'AL

(PRESSURE)

ALKAB

(THE RACE)

SUPPORTED COUPLING

When a man and a woman support their bodies against each other, and use a wall or a pillar to consummate the coupling, it is called supported coupling".

Kama Sutra. Book II

LUCH
(THE GOURD)

"An ingenious person should multiply the classes of couplings by imitating the different species of beasts and birds. Because, when practiced according to the customs of each country and the particular fantasy of each individual, they can create love, sincere friendship and real respect in the hearts of women."

Kama Sutra. Book II

TAK'YAH NABAL

THE SACRED WAYS OF COUPLING

(*These sacred ways have been adapted from the ancient Indian engravings used to illustrate the Science of Love.)*

LAKET K'IN
YETEL AK'AB
(THE EQUINOX)

HE TRIED TO DO "THE
EQUINOX"
(AND ENDED UP LIKE
A SOLSTICE)

PIKIT
(THE FAN)

CHEB
(THE PENDULUM)

PAYAL CHI'
(THE PRAYER)

IT'S CALLED THAT
BECAUSE YOU END
UP WANTING TO
PRAY.

WOB

(THE PITAHAYA)

IT ALL STARTED
WHEN I WAS PICKING
UP PITAHAYA FRUIT

BABAK'
(THE ENTANGLEMENT)

YOU CAN END UP TANGLED

FOR LIFE

KOKOTHAN
(THE DELIGHT)

AMAZING! IT WAS A PARANORMAL EXPERIENCE.

ETHUN T'ANK'U
(THE PYRAMID)

THE WORST OF IT IS
YOU HAVE TO DO IT
ON TOP OF A PYRAMID

THE
END

"The Maya Sutra was written by the supreme priests when they were immersed in contemplation of the divine. It was written in accordance with the precepts of the divine writings and for the good of the world".

Kama Sutra.